Freshwater
Baits

FISHING STEP BY STEP

Freshwater Baits

with

Ken Whitehead

CASSELL
LONDON

CASSELL & COMPANY LIMITED
35 Red Lion Square, London WC1R 4SG
and at Sydney, Auckland, Toronto, Johannesburg,
an affiliate of
Macmillan Publishing Co., Inc.,
New York.

First published 1976

ISBN 0 304 29746 1

Printed by Ian Allan Printing Ltd.

INTRODUCTION

If you can put a rod together, use a reel and handle a landing net, then these books are your next need. With this series of books the angler is given the chance of seeing just how the expert goes about catching the fish that have made his name a household word in the world of fishing.

Peter Mohan has used his unique knowledge of angling personalities to select the right angler for each book, and then edited the series as a whole.

Ken Whitehead has spent days at the water with the experts, patiently filming and planning every photograph so that each picture shows in detail where, when and how the many tasks are approached.

Study the pictures and compare your methods, your tackle and your whole approach to fishing. This is how you will gain the confidence that brings success.

Whilst the books in themselves are interesting to read, they are also a programmed technique that is progressive. With careful study the new angler, or one wishing to improve his angling will learn how each skill at the water should be tackled, and by re-reading he will be able to adopt the expert's way of tackling every situation.

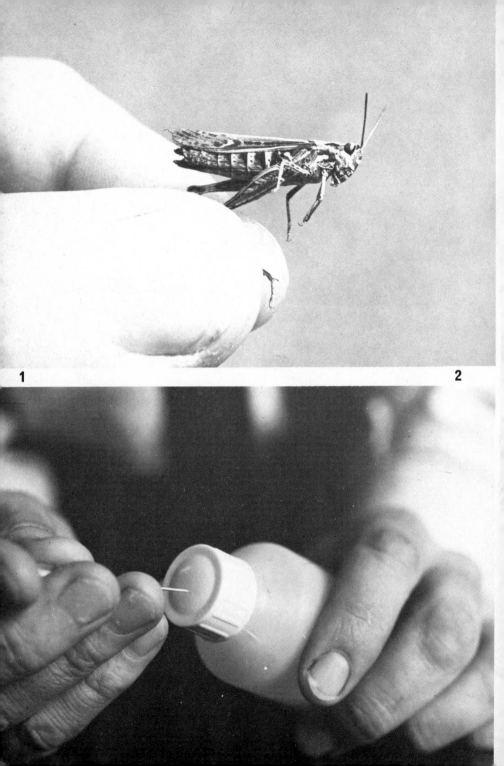

1

2

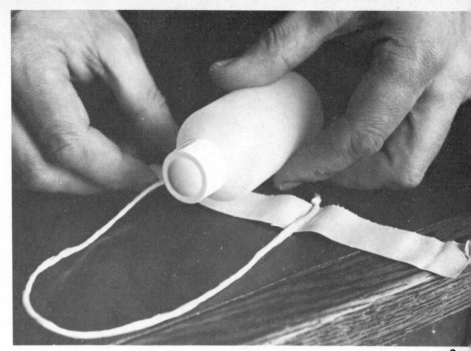

Grassshoppers

1 Although much valued as a bait in America, grasshoppers are seldom used in this country. Many fish will take them as a summer bait — either on the surface (chub, dace etc) or in mid-water (roach, carp, perch etc).

2 They should be kept in a small plastic bottle with holes pierced in the top so that they can be released one at a time.

3 Make a knot in both ends of a length of string, and tape this to the body of the bottle, forming a handle.

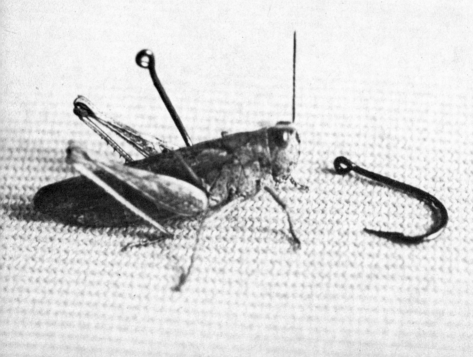

4 Now the bottle, with baits inside, can be hung from your belt ready for use whether you are wading or stalking fish along the bank. Keep the bottle out of direct sunlight.

5 Small hooks can be mounted through the body, just behind the back legs. Make sure the legs can move though — this is what attracts the fish.

6 Under bushes, trees and bridges, beside overhanging banks — all are good places to fish with grasshoppers. But remember to keep low, and quiet.

7

8

Freshwater mussels

7 There are several kinds of mussel, the most common being the swan mussel. Search for them in the shallows of rivers, lakes and gravel pits. They lie half-buried in the bottom, standing on edge.

8 This picture shows what they look like. The end of the shell, standing out of the bed, is often weed covered and difficult to spot.

9 Open the mussel by sliding a strong knife carefully into the hinged back of the shell.

10

11

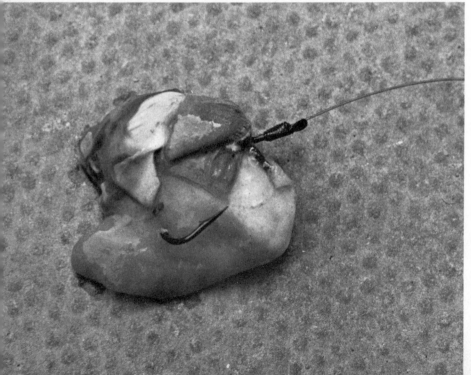

10 With both shells parted, the foot, shown in the right-hand half, can be scooped out with the knife.

11 Use a large hook on which to mount the bait, and keep the shells, which can be ground and mixed with groundbait as an added attraction.

12 Never keep mussels in water — they soon die and rot. Store them in damp weed, and keep them cool. Remember this is a bottom bait that attracts carp, tench, bream and chub.

14

15

Crayfish

13 A bait that brings in big fish every year. These freshwater lobsters live in holes along the bank, crevices along lock walls, and supports of bridges. They are caught with a drop net.

14 Fresh bait is the only sure way of attracting crayfish. Here a portion of lights from the butcher has been tied into the bottom of the net.

15 Lower the net, leave it for five minutes or so — and bring it up quickly. Crays that have climbed on to the net are trapped.

16

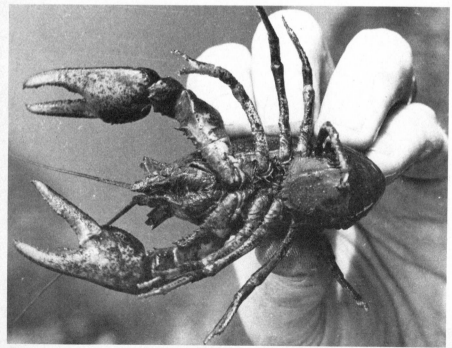

17

16 Make no mistake — the ferocious lobster-look of the cray is not bluff. He can pinch hard with those claws.

17 Hold him behind the head, between finger and thumb, with your hand over his body. This way your fingers are safe.

18 Store baits in damp weed overnight and keep them cool.

19

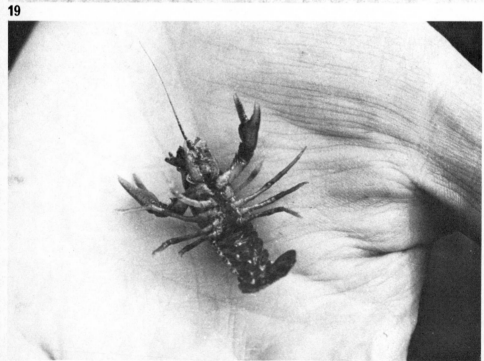

20

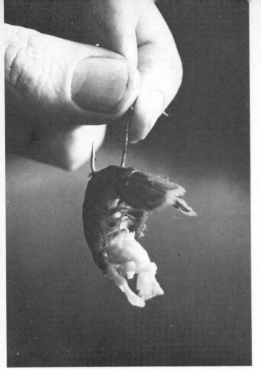

21

22

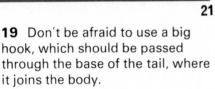

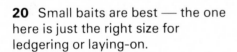

19 Don't be afraid to use a big hook, which should be passed through the base of the tail, where it joins the body.

20 Small baits are best — the one here is just the right size for ledgering or laying-on.

21 Just about the most attractive bait is the tail section from a whole dead crayfish. This is best broken from a large bait, and mounted on a large hook.

22 Sardine or pilchard oil added to dead crayfish also help to advertise the bait. Immerse them overnight. Keep the bait on the move.

23

24

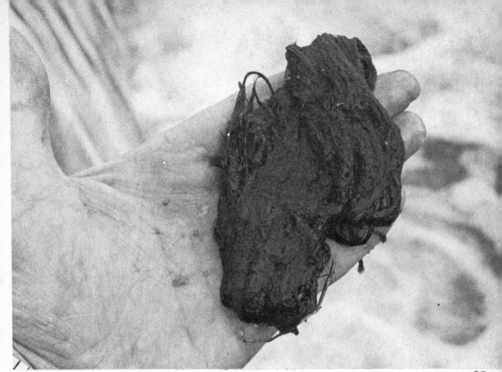

Silkweed

23 Hot summer days when all
baits have failed, and fish
themselves are completely off feed
are the times when silkweed
comes into its own. Here in the
weirpool good fish will be feeding
on it as it breaks away and drifts
downstream.

24 Silkweed grows on supports of
bridges, locks, and weirs at, and
below water-level.

25 The whole attraction of the
weed probably lies in a host of
small snails and insect life that
lives within the green fronds; so
handle it as little as possible.

26

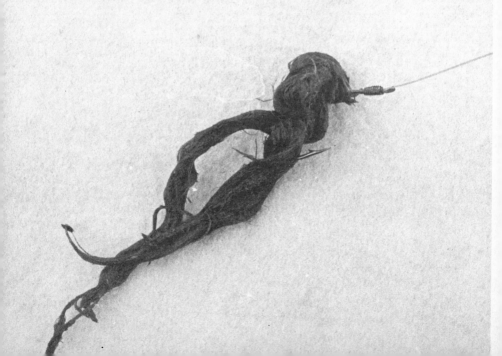

27

26 Gently strip off enough for a day's fishing, and keep it in a can of water.

27 Bait the hook by inserting it into the ball of weed, twist the weed round, and pull it free. Don't try to squeeze it on to the hook, and make sure that you mount a big bait, not a tiny twist that can be missed in disturbed water.

28 Cast into, and keep the bait in, a strong current. Use a big float, keep a tight line and you will not only see, but feel, a fish take.

Potatoes

29 Normally used as a 'carp only' bait, the small new potato will also take tench, bream, roach and chub.

30 Potatoes are easy to prepare and carry. Leave the skins on, and boil in a clean saucepan of water.

31 Boil until they are just, and only just, soft. Use the fork test. If the fork slides in very easily then the potato is too well cooked.

32 Peel, or rather scrape, the potato carefully. I push the end of a disgorger into mine and find that this holds them firmly whilst I scrape.

33 A baiting needle allows the line, then the hook to be pulled through without crushing the bait.

34 Expensive — but time saving. Small tinned potatoes are ideal, ready peeled and in need of very little cooking.

Hempseed

35 Prohibited for years, hemp
seed is now universally accepted.
It is a bait that produces a style of
fishing of its own. Once those little
seeds hit the water fish grab
quickly. The roach pole, shown
here in use on the River Lea, is one
weapon that produces a strike
quick enough to hook roach and
dace on hemp.

36 Good hemp is big and clean. It
is sold at tackle shops by the pint
or pound, and needs cooking.

37

38

37 Pour a pint of hemp into a saucepan of water, and bring to the boil.

38 Now turn it down to simmer gently, and add a teaspoon of sugar to sweeten.

39 A teaspoon of soda will intensify the blackness of the grains.

40

41

40 Simmer until the white seed kernel just, and only just, shows.

41 Strain, wash in cold water to stop the cooking action . . .

42 Store in an airtight box, to keep the grains moist.

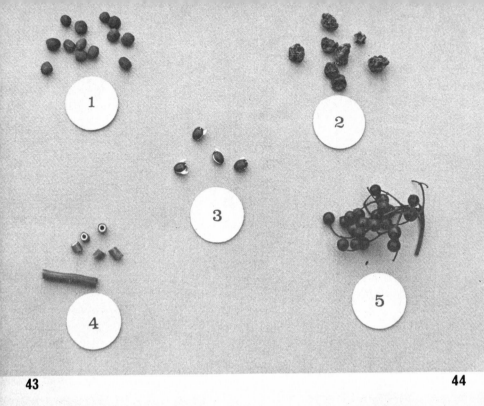

43

44

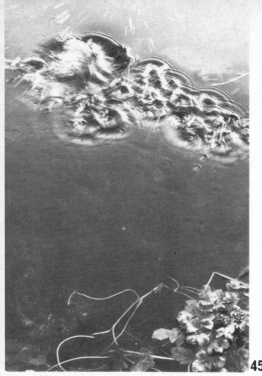

43 Although hemp can be mounted on to a small hook, most anglers use a bigger hook bait resembling hemp, hoping that a bigger bait will produce slower bites. Shown here are:
1. Tares. 2. Currants. 3. Artificial hemp — purchased from a tackle shop. 4. Electrician's cable, black on the outside, white inside. 5. Elderberries.

44 Hemp makes a combination bait with wheat, maggots, bread etc — in fact, any hookbait which needs a general groundbait.

45

45 Avoid overbaiting with loose hemp. Here the angler is using too much.

46 Here just the correct amount has been thrown in. A few seeds every fourth or fifth cast is enough to get fish to feed without overfeeding and putting them off.

46

47

500 ml   HK8R

Formaldehyde Solution B.P.

Formalin

! Warning: Avoid inhaling the vapour. Avoid contact with the eyes, skin and clothing. !

POISON. Not to be taken

If this preparation becomes turbid, keep in a warm place

Keep out of the reach of children

THE BOOTS COMPANY LTD. NOTTINGHAM ENGLAND

48

Preserving baits

47 Winter fishing presents bait problems. In these months it is useful to have preserved baits on which the angler can rely to ensure a good day's sport. There are many ways of preserving, but here are shown the easiest and quickest methods.

48 The most common way to preserve baits is by using formalin. It can be bought quite cheaply at the chemist, but IT IS A POISON, and should be treated as such.

49 Use separate jugs, spoons and jars for preserving purposes, and keep them away from human contact at all times.

50

51

50 Elderberries are a wonderful summer bait, either on their own or with hempseed, but they are not available in winter months. The sensible angler preserves his own, and the formalin treatment is an excellent way of doing it.

51 Gather bunches of berries, clip out the thick stems, and place them in a Kilner jar.

52 Now measure 1 dessertspoonful of formalin into a jug, and add a pint of cold water.

53

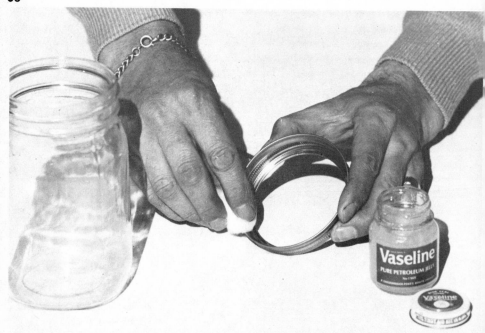

54

On jar labels in image: KILNER; CRAYFISH 1975; ELDERBERRIES '74

53 Cover the berries with the mixture.

54 Before sealing, rub the inside of the metal ring with vaseline to prevent corrosion.

55 Seal, and label the bottle. THEN THOROUGHLY WASH HANDS, JAR, SPOONS, and lock away the formalin bottle.

56

57

Preserving Crayfish

56 Crayfish are easy to preserve, and useful for winter months when they are difficult to trap. Pack them head downwards into a Kilner jar.

57 Now cover with a formalin solution as for elderberries.

58 After one week empty this solution and refill with one made from one teaspoon of formalin added to a pint of cold water.

GENUINE
FULL STRENGTH
CORNISH
PILCHARD OIL

59 Before use wash thoroughly, and pack into a polythene box with the tails set straight.

60 Any taint of formalin can be removed by covering the baits with pilchard oil shortly before use.

61 One final word about crayfish. Many people believe they live only in dirty water, and feed on carrion. The reverse is true. Look for crayfish in the cleanest water, and use a fresh, clean bait in your trap.

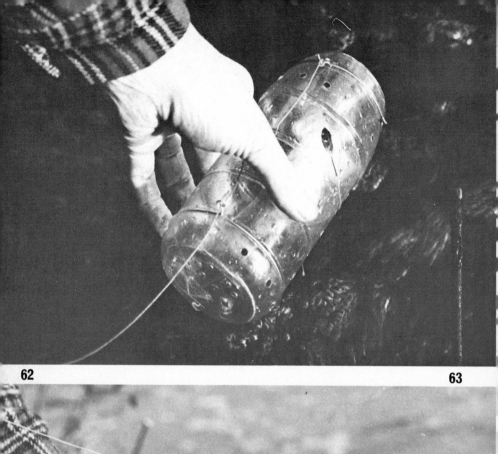

62

63

Livebaits

62 There are few fish that will not eat one smaller than themselves. Even the supposedly vegetarian roach has been caught on a small minnow intended for a chub. Catching livebait can be a problem. The easiest way is with a trap, and here a manufactured minnow trap is being set, mouth to the stream, in running water.

63 Before setting, a small piece of bread is forced into the trap to act as a bait.

64 Other traps that can be used are a baited drop net, mentioned earlier. A jam-jar with a plastic funnel through which fish swim but cannot return can be purchased for a few pence at a tackle shop. Finally, a home-made minnow trap made from a wine bottle is shown.

65

66

67

65 To make a wine bottle trap knock the hollow base from the bottle with a hammer and punch.

66 This close-up shows the sides of the base left when the bottom is removed.

67 Now a piece of gauze is tied round the neck — allowing a passage of water through the bottle.

68 A string loop and drop cord complete the trap. It is set here in still water against weed beds.

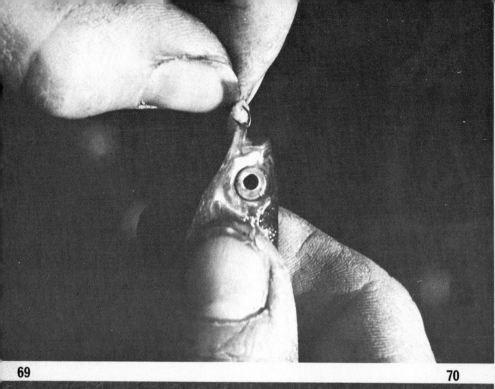

69 If you catch livebait with rod and line remember to remove the barb from the hook. The less baits are handled the longer they last.

70 Bait buckets are either canvas and used for bank carrying, or as is shown in the front of the picture, plastic, with a sealed lid and capable of being carried without spilling. Cut an inside lid from foam plastic and drop this on the water before fastening the lid — this not only stops slopping, but helps aerate the water.

71 If you want to carry baits a short distance in hot weather, slip them into a Thermos flask half-filled with water, screw down the lid — and pop the flask into your pocket. Your movements along the bank will aerate the water and keep the baits fresh.

Deadbaits

72 Winter. Pike fishing deadbait.
The average angler can buy what
he needs at a fishmonger's shop.
But pike can be just as choosy as
roach. A variety of baits can make
all the difference to a day's sport.

73 Mackerel, herrings and sprats.
These are usually available from
the fishmonger — and the sensible
angler picks undamaged fish that
are fresh. Old fish quickly break
away from the hooks during
casting.

74

75

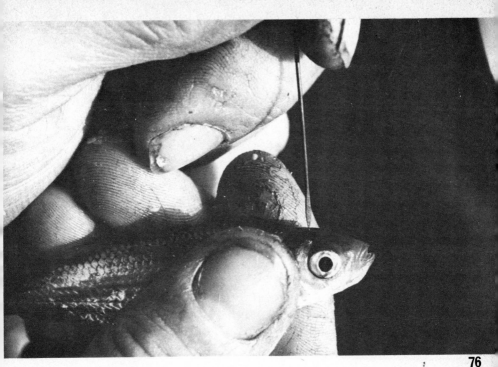

74 Dace, chub, roach, rudd, gudgeon and bleak are the most used freshwater deadbaits, and their popularity lies in roughly that order.

75 If you are going to preserve deadbaits, keep them alive until the last possible moment, and remember to handle them as little as possible.

76 Kill them by piercing a baiting needle into the back of the head, and wrap them carefully in a damp cloth for the homeward journey.

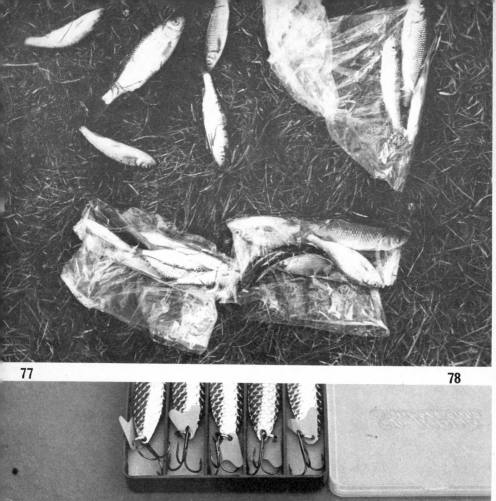

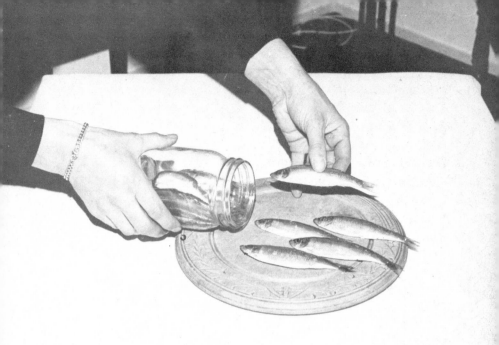

77 Deep-frozen baits will lump
together. It is a good idea to sort
various fish into half-dozens and
then packet them. Frozen this way
a packet will contain a variety of
baits, and save chipping fish from
frozen blocks, with possible
damage.

78 Whilst formalin-preserved
baits are considered inferior to the
fresh for deadbaiting, they make
tough, attractive baits that can be
mounted and spun.

79 Preserving is simple. Pack the
baits head down in a Kilner jar, and
fill with the formalin solution
described earlier. Change to a
weaker solution after they have
been stored for a week.

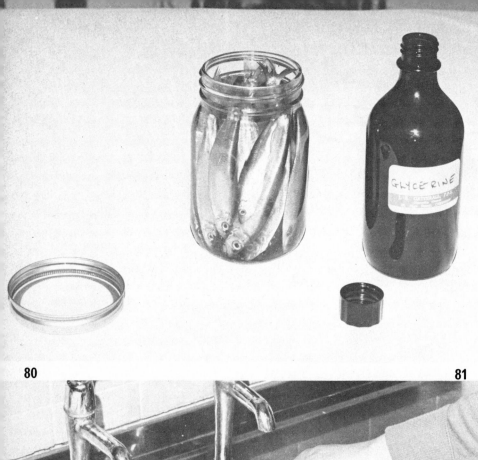

80

81

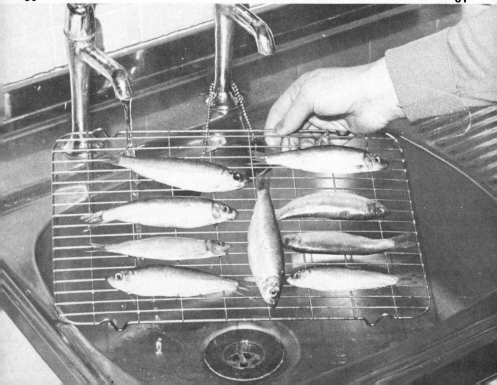

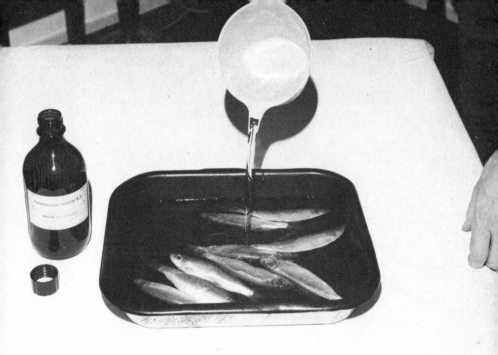

80 Baits can also be preserved
with glycerine — again obtainable
at a chemist's shop.

81 With this method it is
necessary to wash the baits
carefully.

82 They are then placed in a flat
tray, and covered with a solution of
one dessertspoonful of formalin to
a pint of cold water.

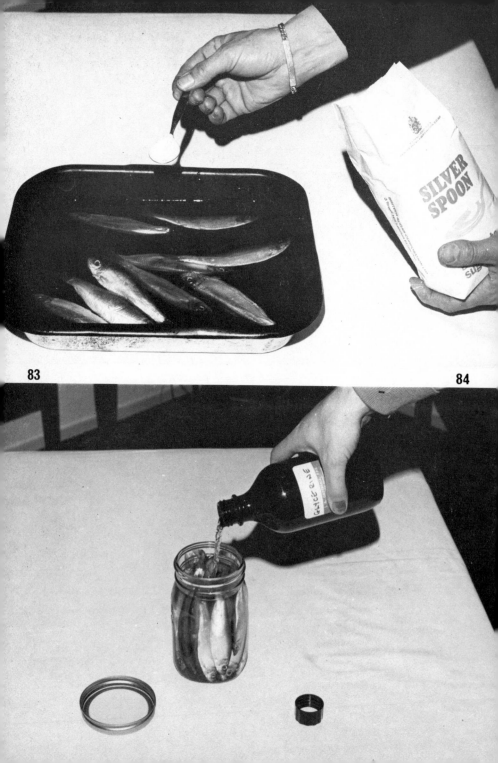

83

84

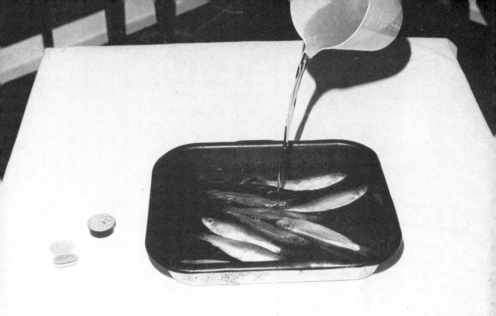

83 After 24 hours remove from this solution, and wash. Then immerse them again in a solution of one part sugar to eight parts of water. Cover the dish with a clean cloth, and leave exposed to the air for three days. This removes the taint of formalin.

84 Finally, pack into screw-top jars and cover with glycerine. When baits are required they merely need washing before use.

85 Golden sprats are a great alternative to silver ones. To prepare them, remove as many scales as possible, and immerse them in a warm solution of dye. I use Dylon Gold A22.

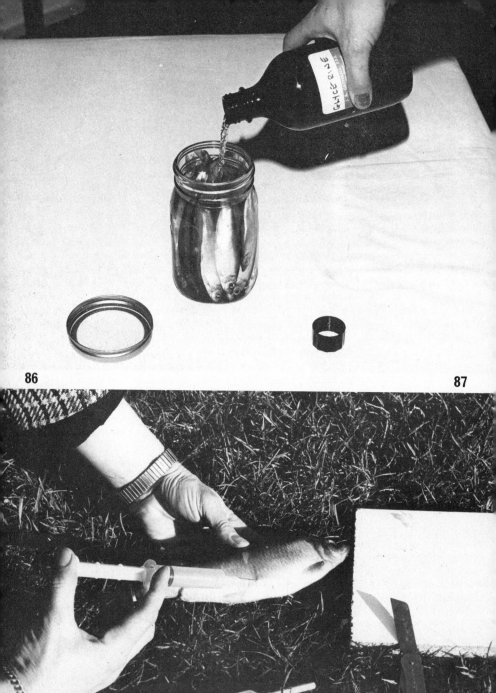

86 When they have taken on a deep gold colour, remove and preserve as described above.

87 Deadbaits injected with air can be made to float just above the bottom, or in mid-water depending on how much air is injected into the stomach.

88 Finally, oil from pilchards, sardines etc can make the most attractive deadbait even better. Try this method when deadbaiting for eels!

89

90

Wheat

89 Wheat — a wonderful year-round bait. It can be purchased ready-cooked and preserved, although this is expensive. It can be easily prepared, and a pound weight is enough for most days.

90 Cover the grains with water or milk, and stew until the white kernel of the wheat just shows.

91 Wash under a cold tap to stop the cooking action, and store in an airtight box.

92

93

92 This picture shows: 1. Properly cooked wheat. 2. Overcooked wheat. Overcooked grains are better used as groundbait.

93 Another method of cooking is to half-fill a vacuum flask with grains, fill with boiling water, and leave overnight. The bait will be ready-cooked in the morning.

94 Wheat is another bait that dries out quickly. If this happens it will float—and you will lose fish out of the swim. Better to dampen it on arrival at the bank.

95

96

Rice

95 Tiny, but first rate, especially in coloured water. There are two kinds of rice, long- and round-grained. Long is the hook bait size, round is best for groundbaiting.

96 Rice is easy to boil, or prepare by the vacuum flask method described for wheat. Remember to only half-fill the flask.

97 When it is cooked, cool the rice by laying it out in a tray. Cold water cooling will make it lump.

98

99

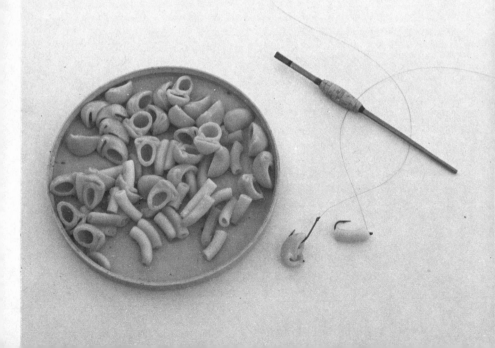

Macaroni

98 An excellent float fished bait that accounts for roach, chub, bream, tench and carp. Break into small strips, boil in milk, and allow to cool.

99 There is a variety of macaroni on the market made in the shape of small snails. Whilst I am not suggesting that the fish will take this as a 'natural', its shape gives wonderful movement. Don't be afraid to use a big hook, and if you are using 'tube' macaroni remember to thread this on to the hook from the eye end first.

100 There is no need to use macaroni as a groundbait — this fish was caught with hemp groundbait, but maggots and casters are also good.

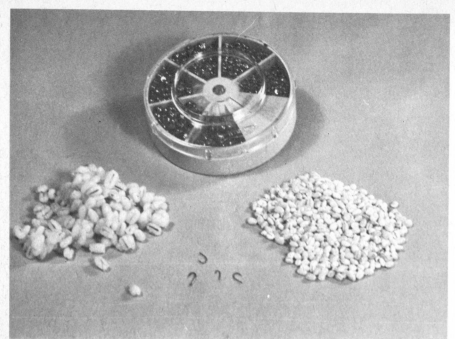

101

102

Pearl barley

101 So small that many fishermen ignore it, yet a good bait when properly prepared. Pearl barley is another cereal bait that works all the year round in every swim.

102 Cover with water or milk, and stew gently until the kernel just shows.

103 Having cooked gently, store in an airtight box and use it in the same way as wheat.

104 Discovered and used as a hookbait by the hemp expert, tares are now used for catching roach, dace and chub where many other baits fail. Here they are shown uncooked (left) and cooked.

105 They need long and careful cooking — simmer in water and watch carefully as the outer skin swells. Too much cooking, and they burst.

106 Cool, and either store separately or mix with hempseed.

Snails

107 Free for the searching, and
easy to keep and use. Perhaps
fishermen think that fish won't eat
snail shells, because they are not
used very often. But believe me,
they do. Search bunches of weed
carefully in small streams.

108 There are several types of
snail, and all are good baits. Hooks
can be eased through the soft
piece of body at the shell opening,
or through the wall of the shell
itself.

109 Keep them in wet weed and be careful not to let the box stand in the sun.

110 Those that cannot be used in one day can be kept in a suitable jar with a little weed for several days. Keep the jar from direct sunlight.

111 Watch also for freshwater shrimps — shown here with a few snails. Mounted on a very small hook they make excellent baits for practically every fish.

113

114

Luncheon meat

112 Another bait that has become popular in the last few years. Luncheon meat has taken large barbel, bream, tench and chub and is now recognised as a standard ledgering bait on many rivers.

113 There are several brands of luncheon meat. I have found that the more expensive ones contain more meat than fat, and hold better on the hook.

114 A cutting board, knife, and towel to keep hands clean are needed.

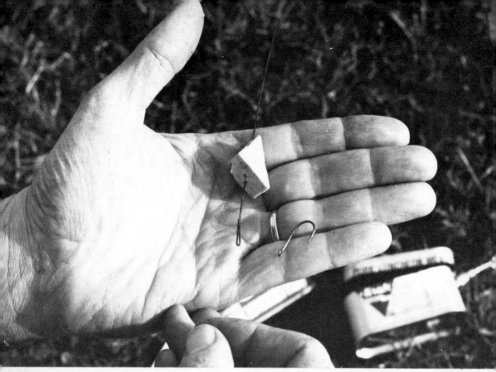

115

116

117

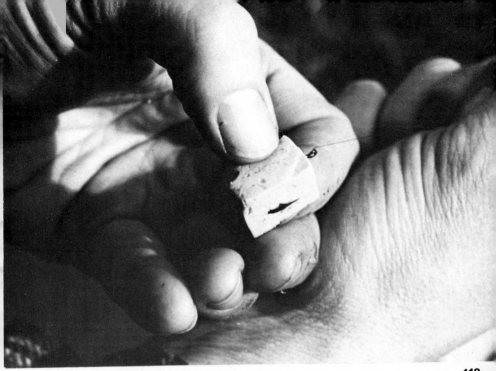

115 A baiting needle passed through the bait, pulling the hook into the cube ensures that it will remain firm, and not be lost when a cast is made.

116 Very small pieces can be cut up for groundbait.

117 Throw them well upstream of where you are fishing as they tend to float.

118 Above all make sure that part of the point and barb of the hook show. Otherwise the bait will 'pad' the strike.

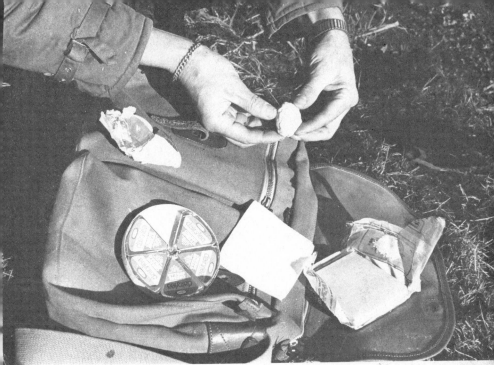

Cheese

119 Few fish turn up their noses at cheese — and there are enough different sorts to encourage even the most timid feeder.

120 Soft cheeses are moulded into a ball and mounted directly on to the hook.

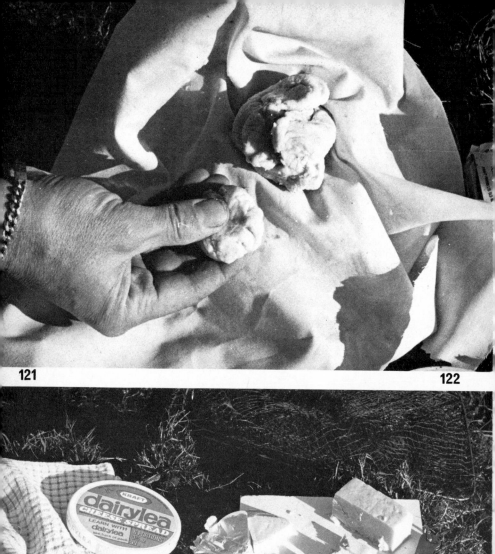

121 They can also be combined with firm bread paste to make a stiffer bait that will cling well to the hook — very necessary in distance casting.

122 Hard cheeses are cut into cubes and then mounted in the same way as luncheon meat, by using a baiting needle.

123 Cheese for groundbait can be shredded directly into the bag with a grater, and thoroughly mixed before being thrown into the swim.

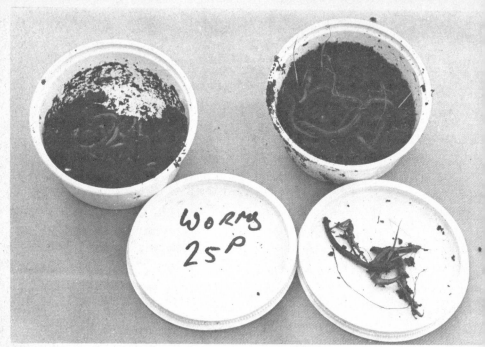

124

125

126

Worms

124 The best standby — a bait carried by every angler and used when all else fails. The vast majority of anglers buy worms at the tackle shop, and although there are several kinds only two really concern the angler: lobworms and brandlings.

125 Brandlings are small, thin, red worms with light yellow stripes. Dig for them in old manure and compost heaps.

126 Lobworms are large, thick and pink in colour. They can be dug in the garden during fine weather.

127 An easier way to get lobworms is to water a close-cut lawn at dusk, and they will come to the surface.

128 Trap the worm with one finger when you see it. Once trapped it can be eased up from the ground. A direct grab usually means a broken worm.

129

130

131

132

129 Lobworms can be encouraged into a corner of the garden by soaking an area with water, and then laying down a sack or plastic bag, and covering it with straw. The moist earth under the sack holds them, even in frosty weather.

130 A 'wormery' is not difficult to make. Here an old sink with the plug fixed in is filled with leaf mould on top of an old sack. Worms can be stored in the mould, the sink covered — and a stock of worms is available throughout the year. Water occasionally in summer, and protect from frost in winter.

131 Worms needed for fishing should be transferred into moss several days before use to scour them. Moss can be bought from a florist for a few pence.

132 A little milk added to the moss helps to scour and toughen the worms.

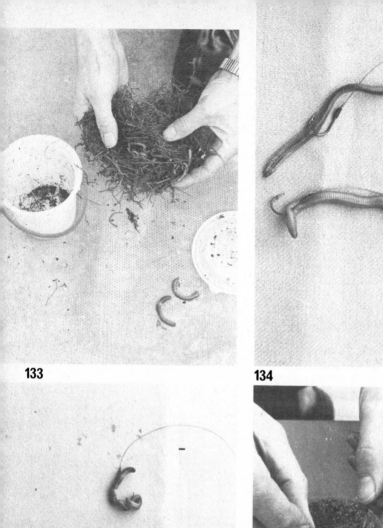

133

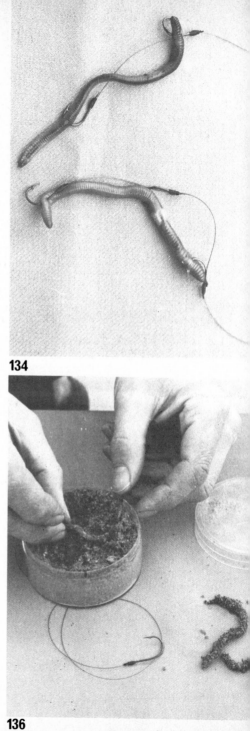

134

135

136

133 Turn out the moss every day and remove any dead worms.

134 Two hook rigs for mounting worms. The one above, called a Stewart tackle, uses two hooks. That below with three hooks is a Pennel tackle. Both rigs are excellent for perch fishing.

135 Four other ways of mounting worms; top to bottom they are: 1. Completely threaded. 2. Part threaded. 3. Head mounted. 4. Tail only.

136 Hooking worms can be messy — a small box of sand into which they can be dipped before mounting eases the job considerably.

137 Worms dipped in fish oil have a special attraction — but do it on the bank. Do not mix oil with the moss in advance as it will kill the worms.

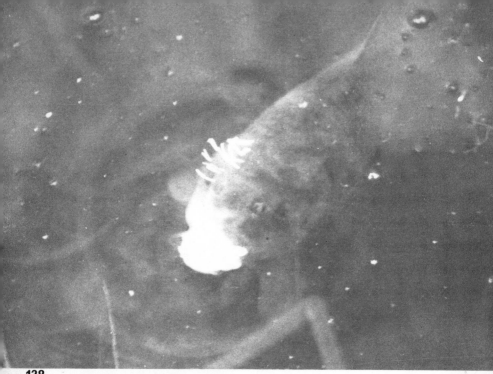

138

139

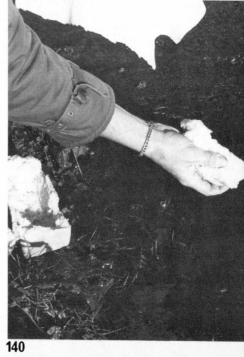

140

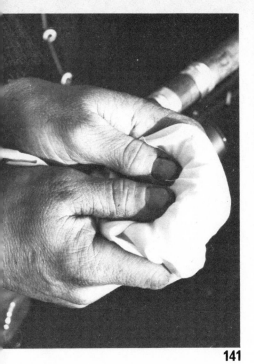

141

142

Bread

138 Bread — an all round bait. One loaf will provide a complete day's sport, and allow the angler to ring the changes with several styles. This carp in the picture is intent on a piece of crust, torn from the loaf and fished on the surface.

139 Bread paste is made by removing the inside of the loaf.

140 It is dipped once into water, and squeezed to remove excess water.

141 Now it can be moulded in a clean rag . . .

142 . . . until it is stiff.

143

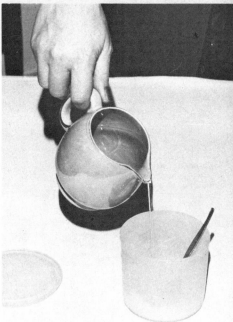

144

143 Flour paste is made with plain flour in a small bowl.

144 Add water and mix until the dough is stiff.

145 Sweetening and colour can be provided with sugar and blancmange powder.

146 Crust is an old favourite and, although it takes time to prepare it, is well worth the effort. First cut the base from a tin loaf.

147

148

149

150

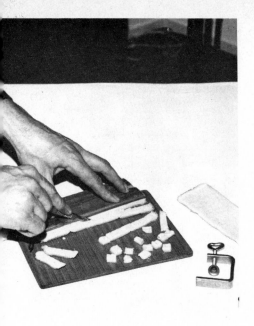

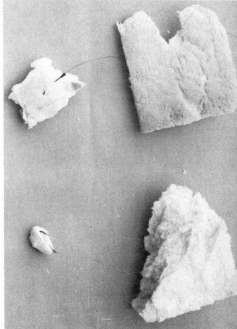

151

152

147 Wrap it in a wet cloth.

148 Place it between two flat boards.

149 Squeeze tight with carpenters' clamps.

150 Leave overnight.

151 On the following day cut into strips and then cubes and triangles. Triangles move well in the water — an added attraction.

152 Above, the upper portion of the loaf is shown mounted for use as floating crust. Below is shown the soft centre, squeezed on to the hook for use as flake. Remember to let the point of the hook show.

153

154

155

Gentles

153 Gentles — housefly maggots — are a very popular bait. Few anglers breed them; most purchase them from a tackle dealer.

154 When bought they need working on if they are to be at their best on the hook. The first step is to sieve them, removing any sawdust packing.

155 There is an excellent sieve on the market that makes this easy — fill the top jar, and they clear themselves as they work into the bottom one.

156 Once separated they should be turned on to fine sand, and then left to work through this for a day or two.

157 Sand is now sieved from the maggots, which are now polished, and nearly free from grease — essential if they are to sink in water.

158 To make sure that all grease is removed the maggots are now washed . . .

159 . . . and dried on a towel.

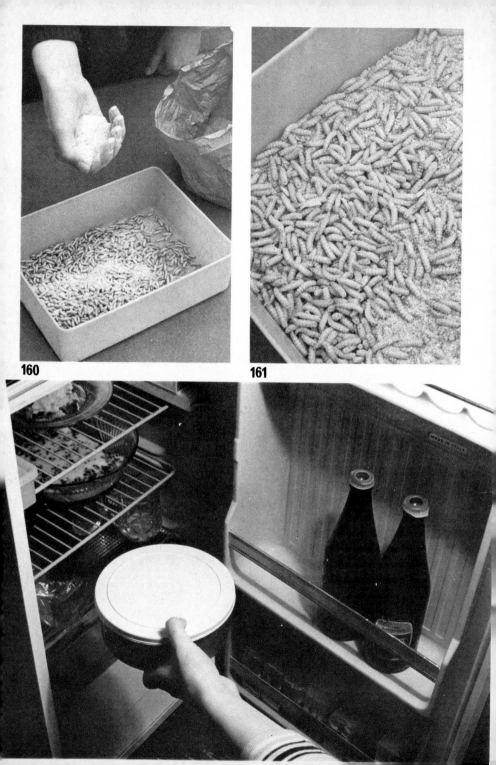

160

161

160 Breadcrumbs or bran are added to the dry maggots.

161 These are now stored in a ventilated tin, away from all heat.

162 A corner of the fridge is ideal.

163 Coloured maggots are made by mixing dye with sand or bran, and allowing the maggots to work through this for 24 hours before separating and storing.

166

167

164 Dye can be purchased from the tackle dealer. Chrysoidine R will make orange maggots; Auramine O will make yellow maggots. Rhodamine B produces red, and Bismarck Brown makes brown maggots.

165 There is only one way of making sure that maggots get right on to the bottom, and that is by using a bait dropper. It is an essential piece of equipment when maggot fishing.

166 Casters, the chrysalid stage of the fly, can be prepared by letting maggots stand in an open box near to heat.

167 It is essential that they are reddish brown in colour, as these shop-bought casters are. Make sure that you inspect the maggots every day.

168 Put them through the sieve
to remove those that have turned.

169 Those casters which have
turned should be put in water and
kept wet until they are used —
otherwise they will float in mid-
water or on the surface.

170 When you get on the bank,
fill the caster box with water, to
keep them from drying out during
the day.

The pictures you have seen show how an expert tackles the preparation of baits. Now go back to the beginning of the book and carefully study each sequence again. Compare the expert's approach with your own, and select what you think will improve your own fishing. Practise your new ideas —- and then try to improve on them.

Always remember that an expert is the angler who constantly analyses his own styles, improves on what he is doing — and then practises until he is perfect.